Frogs speak as boats launch silently
and creep into the morning light
Bright crystal jewels of nighttime glowing
across the surface, reflected in my eyes
How much money to buy these
and yet, always free

Look, here come my friends in V-formation,
gliding, laughing,
honking with pleasure at arriving
And there, a glowing emerald at the front of
a boat with two big rubies behind

What great riches I see
on this black and golden dawn

E.D.L. Productions©

Published by EDL Productions
La Pine, Oregon 97739

Copyright © 2023 by Daniel L. DeGoede, Ph.D.

Photography: Daniel L. DeGoede, Ph.D.
Cover and Design and Style: Eagle Lady Design Studio

All rights reserved. This book may not be reproduced in whole or in part without written permission from the publisher, except by a reviewer who may quote brief passages in a review; nor may any part of this book be reproduced, stored in a retrieval system, or transmitted in any form or by any means, electronic, mechanical, photocopying, recording, or other, without written permission from the publisher.

Library of Congress Control Number: 2023900054

ISBN 978-0-9663745-6-8

Disclaimer

Beliefs for Everyday Life, is educational in nature.
It is designed to offer the reader the opportunity to explore their own beliefs and insights.
It is not designed to substitute for needed medical, psychiatric, or psychological treatment.

First Printing 2022
10 9 8 7 6 5 4 3

BELIEFS FOR EVERYDAY LIFE

Volume II

Heartfelt Words

Daniel L. DeGoede, Ph.D.

Acknowledgements

First, I want to deeply thank Sandy Golden Eagle, (EagleLadyDesignStudio.com) for her amazing help and patience in guiding my words and pictures with creative graphics and designs into the work that you hold in your hand.

Next, I want to thank my daughter Danaë and my granddaughter Judi for assisting in the completion of this book with their creative ideas, support, and encouragement.

And, a special heartfelt thanks to all the family and friends who appear in the pictures taken throughout many years that I have included in this book. Lastly, I acknowledge the help, support and most of all LOVE from my lifetime partner and best friend Judy.

Dedication

This book is dedicated to my four children; Daniel, Danaë, Dana, and Damian, (two of whom have left this space and time early) and to my 15 grandchildren, 21 great grandchildren, and last but of course not least, to my wife, lifetime partner, and best friend of 57 years; Judy.

Believe in yourself and you believe in everyone.

You are process

you are change

you are now

you are the passing moment

you are the stream
before it gets to the ocean

the cloud before it arrives at the sea

the bird before it lands

and the rose while it is blooming

THAT IS WHAT YOU ARE

A loving guiding

acceptance of the self

creates a natural freedom

which creates

complimentary behavior

which recognizes

and supports

the rights of all life

GUILT

is the unconscious controlling
force of society

It is not natural
and it is not part of
our emotional
and biological needs

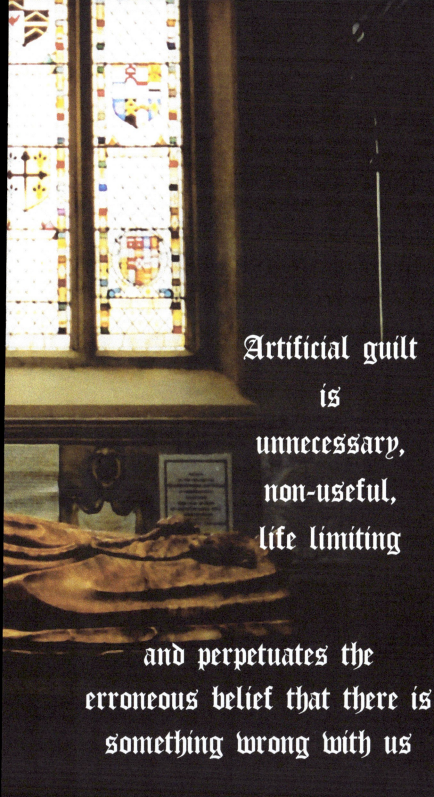

FREEDOM FROM COMPULSIONS MEANS FREEDOM TO...

If your beliefs are
of limitation
then your desires
will continue
unfulfilled

It is only by
exploring
your beliefs
and choosing
those you wish
to have
that you
can find
the answer
to your desires

SEEN CLEARLY
OUR ATTACHMENTS
ARE SHOWN TO BE TRANSITORY
ILLUSIONARY AND SUPERFICIAL

WORSE – THEY TRAP OUR
ATTENTION AND DEPLETE
OUR ENERGY LEAVING
LITTLE LEFT WITH WHICH
TO SAVOR OUR DAILY EXISTENCE

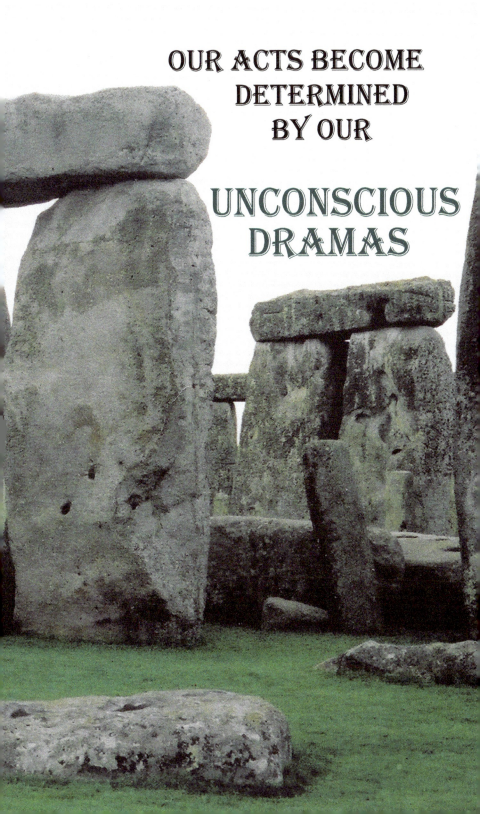

It is inherent in our nature to...

Once early ideas become core beliefs they become Our Reality

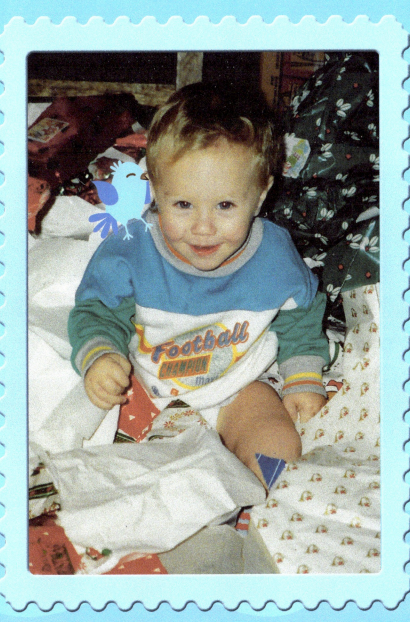

The majority of
GUILT
we feel
is ARTIFICIAL

Love isn't all there is
but LOVE is enough

We often notice so little of our life

*Living within oneself
all is revealed
and no effort is needed*

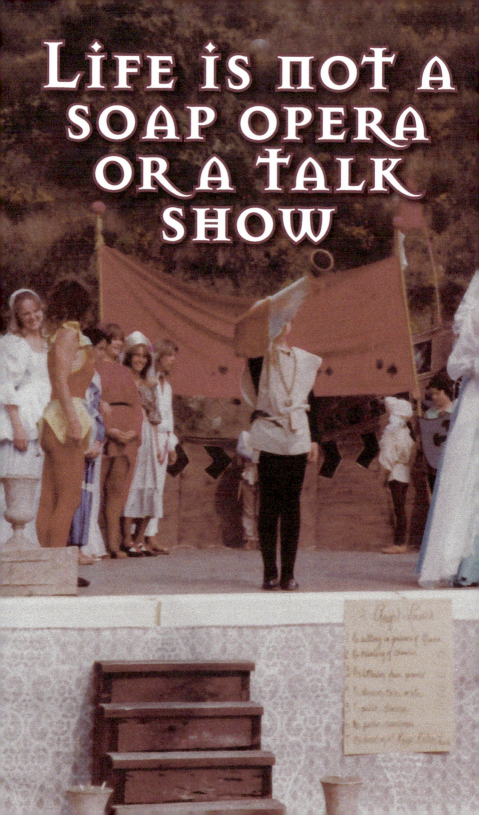

BUT WE LIVE AS IF IT IS

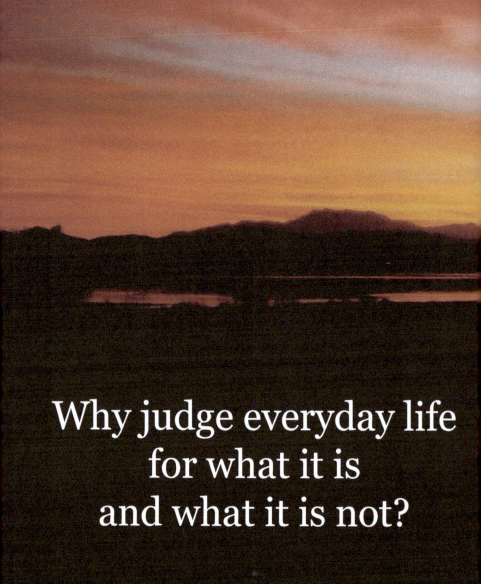

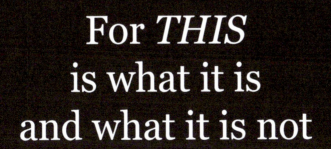

TO BE
IS ENOUGH

to be
more than enough
is to lose being

Before time was known we belonged to the earth

The earth did not belong to us

We will always become

This morning the storm has washed away the sins of man and the earth rejoices for the freshness of this day and gives thanks for a moment's grace

We invent
our daily reality
with our beliefs

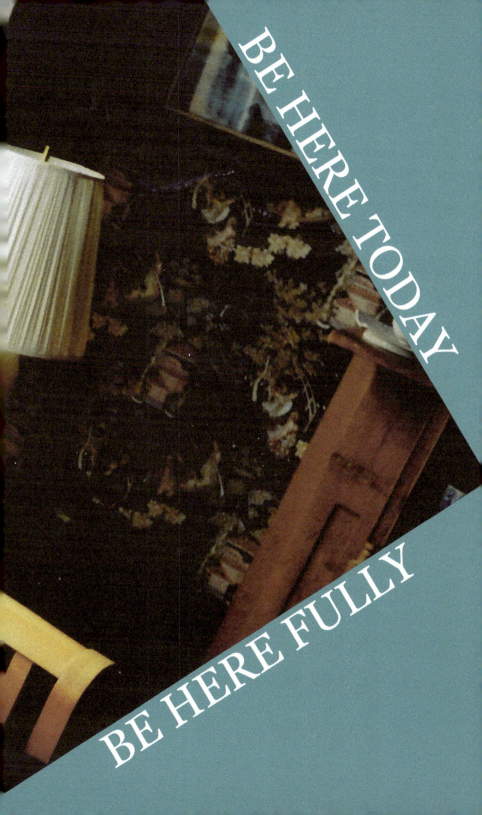

If you don't have any heres

all the theres in the world

will mean nothing to you at all

If you don't like what you see, try on another pair of glasses

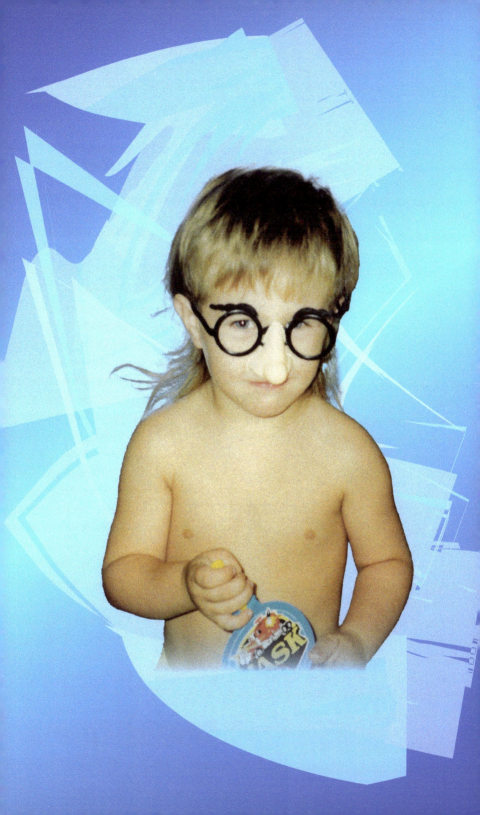

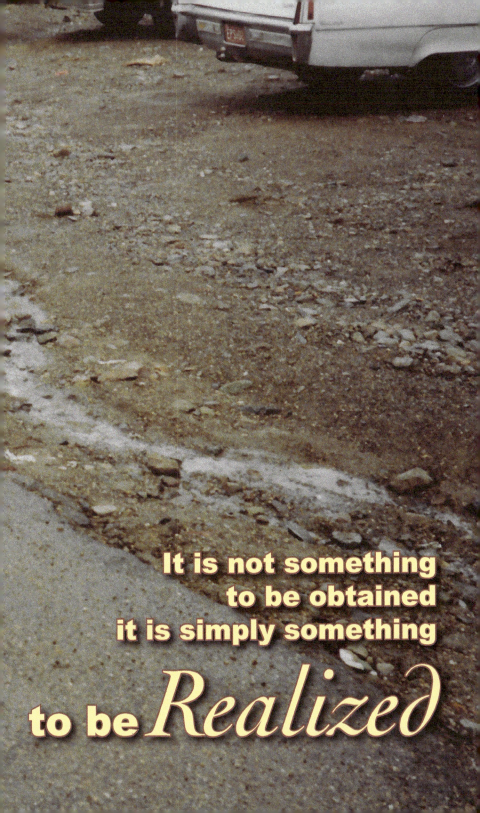

YOU ARE EVERYWHERE

AND YET SEPARATE

CONSTANTLY

AMUSING

AND

AMAZING YOURSELF

WITH REDISCOVERY

Lead with your heart

not your head

We are absolutely
completely and
totally free
at this moment
There is nothing that
needs to be done
By recognizing our
freedom and accepting
our goodness we find
that our free choices
follow our own
movement toward
creativity and
personal fulfillment

The most powerful control

is no control

By its very nature *authority struggles to deny the freedom of others*

THERE ARE NO IMAGES TO CLUTTER THIS **BRIGHTNESS** ONLY NOW AND TIMELESS

We are just as unfree in REBELLION as we are in CONFORMITY

To be true to oneself is to be oneself

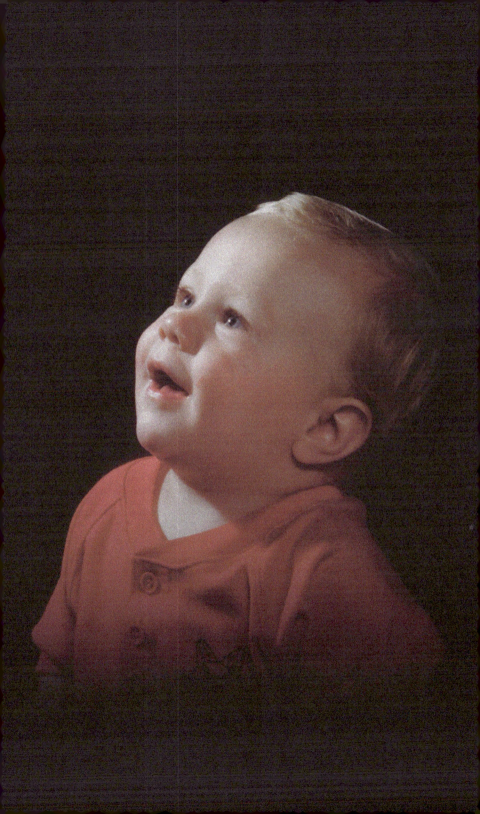

Today birds fly through me
noticing only a shadow of
self as I fly with them in
pursuit of our sameness

I open my wings and
chirp to myself
knowing my birdness

Nothing is
certain anymore

Emptiness is my
only understanding
Eternity my
resting place and
The Now is my sanctuary

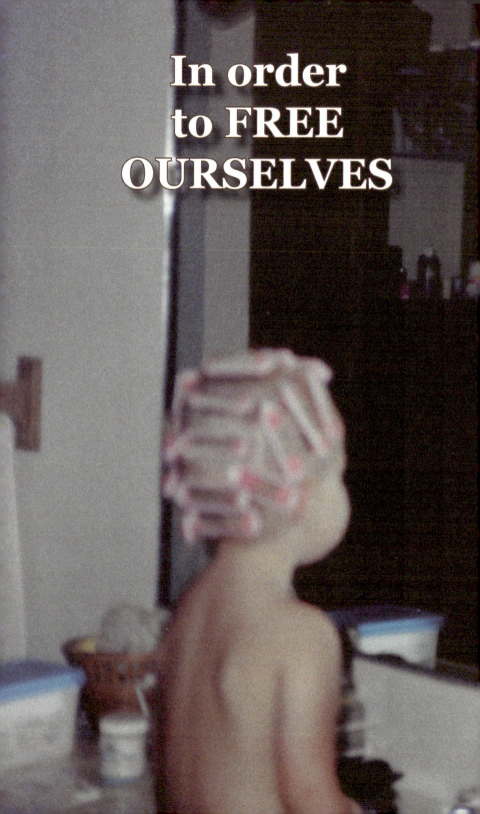

Possibilities emerge from the void and life forms itself openly without regret

When we obsessively examine our
imagination of others' ideas about us,
we are in touch with nothing,
no-thing, no reality

All we have are our own autistic
thoughts about what we think
they think about us—
what we imagine
they imagine — this must mean

Knot after knot after knot;
tying up our daily lives

All based on fantasy

Trust yourself...

and you trust all

Distrust yourself
and you
distrust all

Distrust all
and you live alone

What does it mean to desire nothing?

Desiring nothing is not a state of non-caring or indifference it means you feel sufficient as you are, that you are good enough as you are, in fact, this type of non-attachment creates more involvement not less

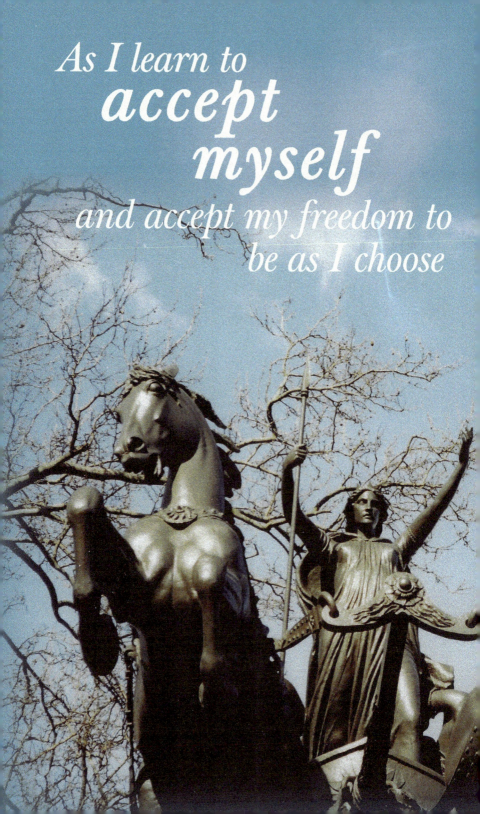

I realize that what is true for me is also true for others

When I attempt through my own needs or desires to control others I violate my own freedom

The attempt to control others is a basic distraction of the principal of free will and the other's diversity

What does it mean to desire nothing?

Desiring nothing means
that you feel sufficient
as you are
that you have recognized
that you are enough

Trusting myself means trusting my body to take care of itself

Quit trying to fix what was never broken and live your life TODAY

See the truth
right now
and free yourself
at this moment!

You were never broken
There is nothing to fix
All the energy
and effort spent
in the obsessive
chronic attempt
to fix yourself
was for nothing!

OPEN YOURSELF
and you will see

this is a moment
OF GREAT BEAUTY

imagine yourself alone and know that it is never true but only in your imagination

LIFE EXISTS . . .

within us
and without us
all the time
constantly
never ending

See life everywhere
around you
feel it within you
see it without you
allow yourself to
experience it
moment to moment
day by day

GOD is change
change is GOD
LIFE is change
change is LIFE
DEATH is change
change is DEATH

The
searching
IS
the problem

We Must Train Children To...

...love themselves
trust their emotions
trust their ideas
and to trust
their
natural behaviors

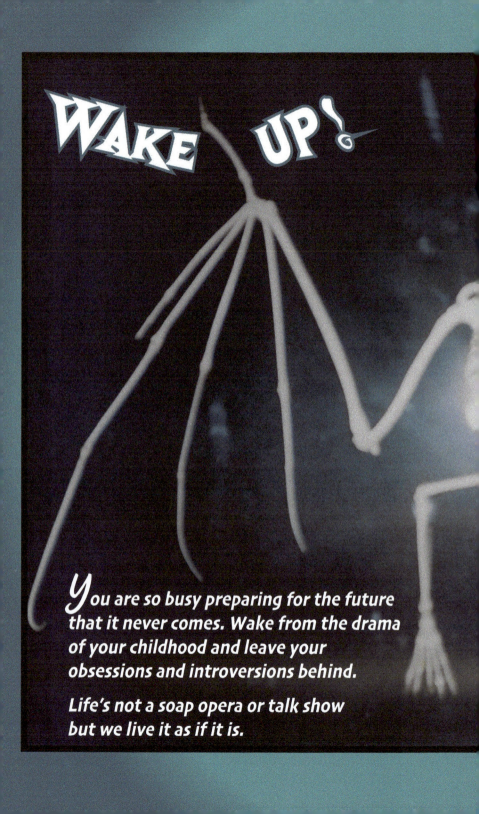

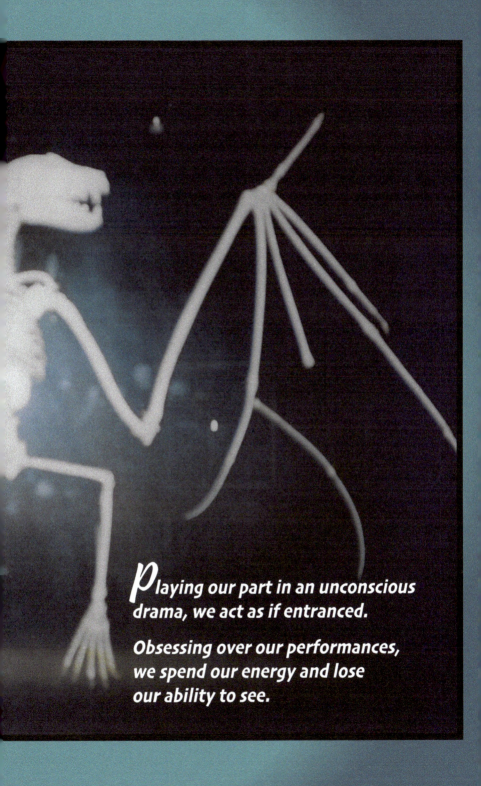

Push too hard

and you end up with something that looks a little smashed

Clouds searching
for a place to land
over my head once again
But then I am
used to their parade
and at least
they bring some
needed shade

THE PARADOX OF LIFE EMBRACES THE PARADOX OF DEATH

THEY ARE AS ONE UNIT THE YIN AND THE YANG OF TOTALITY

There is nothing wrong with us
the way we are
and there is a
way of
understanding this

Its roots go deep within us

Sometimes

I think there is no earth

Only
me and you
and dreams
to hold us through
the night

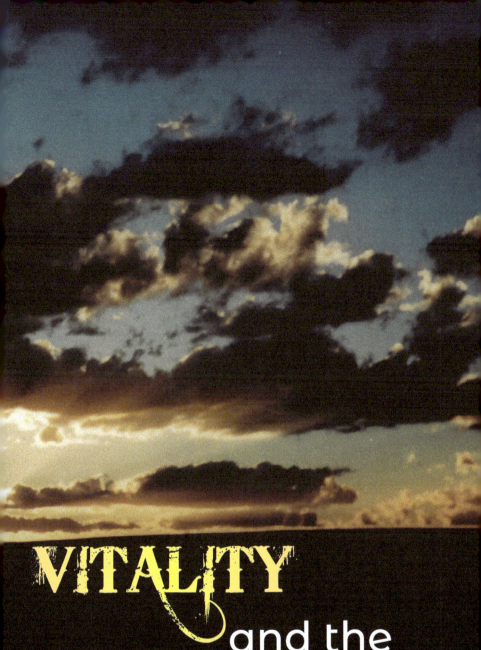

IT IS IN OUR UNIQUENESS THAT WE CAN SEE THE BEAUTY OF OURSELVES

*mountain blossoms
picked just for you!*

WHAT IS IT EXCEPT
THE INNER YEARNINGS
OF THE SOUL
FOR THOSE
FROM WHICH WE HAVE
LOST OUR CONNECTION

FREEDOM
SINGS A SONG
FOR YOU
TO DANCE...
DON'T BE LATE!

It is not
the **DIFFERENCES**
in life which
create
the
problem

It is the
JUDGMENTS
placed on
the **DIFFERENCES**

Is in our successes
and our failures
then where is the meaning?

What is the point?

Perhaps that is the point

Just being here
living our everyday lives
doing what we do
whether it's putting words
on paper or paint on walls

Recognizing that our daily
activities are complete
meaningful and
need no excuses!

The doing is enough

When we accept that we are creating..

...... OUR "BAD" HEALTH

> It becomes clear that by changing our beliefs we can create our **Good Health**

When we attempt
with our intellect
to understand
the natural world

we miss the harmony
which underlies
the conflict our intellect
has chosen to focus upon

If you truly want
to see the world
then close your eyes
and open your heart

WE SEPARATE OURSELVES

from our environment
with our judgments
about our world

I FIND MYSELF REVEALED IN YOUR HEART BUT ONLY IF MINE IS LAID BARE

All those things
you think
you have to do

What will
really happen
if you don't
do them today?

The intellect is a poor guide for the heart

All successful relationships begin with the relationship we have with ourselves

If it is impaired, then the relationships we form with others will also be impaired

To the extent that our relationship with ourselves is functional, caring, loving and accepting, it will be the same in our other relationships

We have been trained to

Look at the natural world and see it as violent and competitive

But the true violence and competition is what we daily do to ourselves and to the world

When you constantly
reassure yourself that
you are ok
you constantly remind yourself
that you don't

In order
to be free
we must
first learn
that we were
not born bad

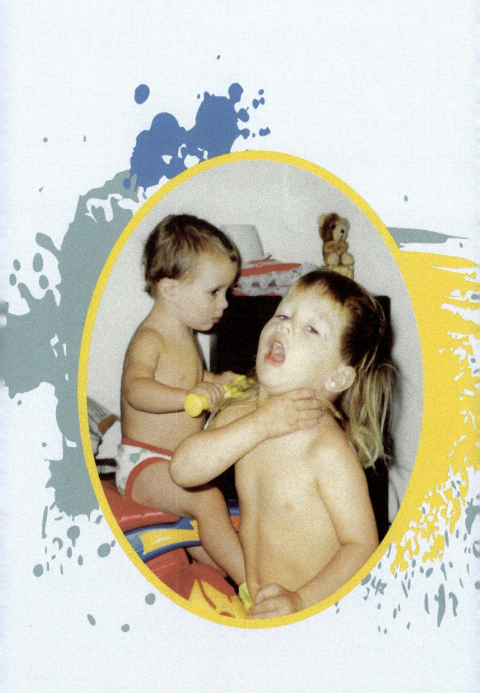

A mild mist is blowing
a gentle song
comes from within

My life
and my heart
become one

The mist softens
my senses and
allows my skin to
enfold a greater life

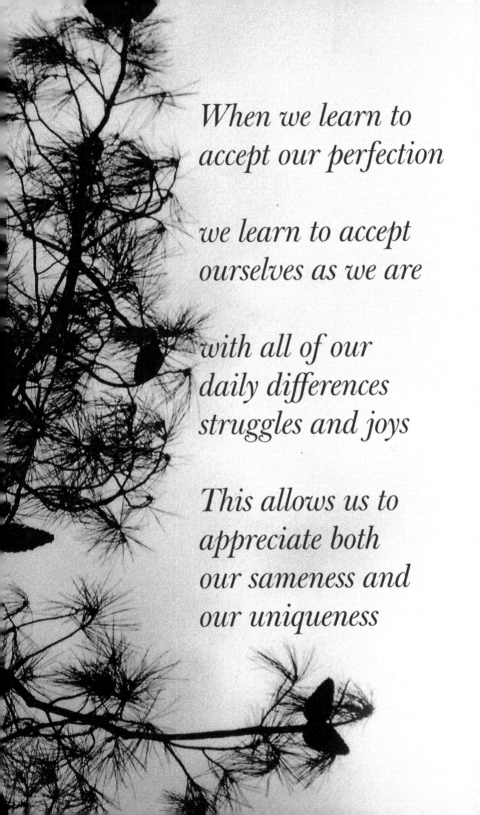

*When we learn to
accept our perfection*

*we learn to accept
ourselves as we are*

*with all of our
daily differences
struggles and joys*

*This allows us to
appreciate both
our sameness and
our uniqueness*

Axioms

Axiom I   I was born perfect. I was born natural, my behaviors, feelings, thoughts, and body were all born good. There is no original sin!

Axiom II   My dysfunctional behaviors, ideas, self-judgement, and artificial guilt are a direct result of limiting beliefs that I have learned. As such, they are wholly and completely changeable at all and any time in my life throughout my life.

Axiom III   I can trust my feelings. No feeling can hurt me or another. Feelings are only "paper dragons." They are meant to be trusted and accepted. It is the behaviors that we do to rid ourselves of feelings that often create our problems.

Axiom IV   By fully accepting ourselves in the present and recognizing we need not fix what was never broken, we free ourselves now from limiting ideas and beliefs of the past. This is the magical approach to life. It is real, truthful, and permanent.

Axiom V   All other methods of growth are simply, "trying to fix what was never broken." They can be useful, time consuming, frustrating, or perhaps, necessary fillers to bring us to the jumping off point of Axiom IV, but they are not Axiom IV.

Axiom VI   When Axiom IV is fully comprehended this releases the body from unnecessary strain, stress, and dis-ease allowing natural physical health and harmony and natural well-being. Acceptance of the self creates and allows acceptance of the body, leading to physical, spiritual, and emotional harmony.

Axiom VII   Physical, spiritual, and emotional harmony allows and promotes choices and freedom. It is not a static ending but rather a fluid beginning.

Axiom VIII   By believing the Axioms of Belief Therapy for myself I recognize that they are equally true for all life, allowing me to live in harmony with myself, others, and my environment.

Introducing a peek into one of Dr. DeGoede's books
about belief therapy, from the book
Finding Freedom in Everyday Life,
Belief Therapy Volume II
This is just one of many chapters that cover everyday life.

CHOICES

Life is a series of choices. The key to feeling free is in recognizing these daily choices as truly *choices*, and not obligations or demands. We create our daily reality as we consciously and unconsciously make both small and large choices.

We can choose to get up at daybreak or sleep until noon. We can choose to go to work or stay home; choose to get married or get a divorce, choose to have children or not. These choices, moment to moment, day by day, week by week and year by year, create the very fabric of our daily lives. Another choice we often don't recognize is the choice to see that we have choices.

When we become aware that every day is filled with choices, then we cease to be victims. Instead, we recognize that we are living in a world filled with freedom. The perception of choice is essential to the self-experience of freedom. When we refuse to see our choices as choices, we experience them as commitments, obligations, restrictions, responsibilities or demands. We then perceive ourselves as victims and others as our victimizers. We lose our sense of freedom and feel imprisoned. However, *feeling* imprisoned is not the same as *being* imprisoned.

Now, the argument of course is; "But you don't understand, I have to work because I have children to feed," or, "You don't understand, I have to steal because there are no jobs," or, "You don't understand, I am in a *real* prison with guards and bars; there are no choices left to me."

Contrary to popular belief, there are choices before these conditions arise and even during these conditions. It is these very choices we have today which then create our future conditions we subsequently experience as either limiting or freeing. We are responsible or "response-able" for both our current and future experiences. Based upon the exercising of our free will through yesterday's, today's and tomorrow's choices, we have created these conditions. We are only victims when we choose to see ourselves as such.

A patient recently said to me, *"But Doctor, you don't understand – I have tried and tried for months. I have these three children and I am forced to live in shelters. Everyone I meet takes advantage of me. They steal what little I have and I am abused at every turn. When I go to Social Services, they tell me I am undeserving and have no rights. So you see, I am helpless, hopeless and a true victim. A victim of the system, a victim of others, and a victim of my society. Even a victim of my past childhood. There is no hope!"*

Upon further questioning, however, it becomes clear that this individual chose to spend what resources she did have with little thought regarding the future consequences. This led to a reliance on others for support. She then chose to approach those others in an aggressive and demanding fashion which pushed them away, once again narrowing her opportunities. This led to more anger and blaming of others, refusal to fill out the necessary forms and unwillingness to follow appropriate procedures to obtain additional aid. She then moved into a shelter where there are many desperate people willing to victimize others, or be victimized by others. Her feelings of abandonment encouraged her to form relationships which quickly became exploitative, once again reinforcing her feelings of being a victim with no choices.

This is a spiraling situation. The more she feels victimized, the less she trusts herself or others, and the fewer perceived choices she sees. The fewer choices she sees, the more victimized and trapped she feels, leading to more of the same, eventually creating a reality of her own making. However, she does not see this all-essential point. After this series of self-created choices and results, she looks at her life and says, "This confirms everything I believe. I truly am a victim and have no choices and none of this can be changed."

She lives in a society that provides multiple human resources. A society that provides financial, social and educational help, and she sees none of this. Therefore, she concludes: "My only choice is suicide."

This bright young woman, who has *chosen* to have children, *chosen* to act in ways that drive away available resources, *chosen* to form exploitative and dysfunctional relationships, and *chosen* options that continually limit both her other choices and her freedoms, eventually hits what she considers to be "rock bottom." She and her children are homeless. She *feels* she has no friends, that everyone is out to take advantage of her, and that there is no help available anywhere. She does *not* see that she has created her situation and that it now reflects all of her limiting beliefs. Instead, she chooses to believe she is a victim with only one option left: suicide. She truly, at this point, *feels* as imprisoned as someone behind real bars.

However, the true prison is her limiting beliefs about the nature of choice and free will. She is the *only* one who holds the keys to this jail. She is the one who locked herself up and the only one who can set herself free!

To take the extreme case, what of those behind real bars? Surely they don't have the same freedom or choices as others? No, but they are not without choices either.

When they wake up to their confinement, they can choose to take responsibility for their situation. Choose to make choices that will help them change that situation as quickly as possible, and choose to make the best of it in the meantime. Or, they can choose to hate every moment and blame others for their present conditions.

They can choose to open their heart or learn to hate. They have the option to form friendships or to avoid them. They have the choice to look deeply into themselves and find what freedom is available to them, or to refuse to know these freedoms and continue to live in a world where they perceive themselves as victims. Victims of an unjust system, victims of unjust people or victims of unjust parents; it all translates the same. You can either choose to see yourself as trapped and victimized by outward circumstances, or choose to believe in your freedom and responsibility.

Inherent within freedom is choice. Without choice, there is no freedom. Without any felt freedom, we are victims of our own choosing.

When you are feeling trapped, take time to look within yourself. Observe the situations and circumstances of your everyday life. Discover the choices you have been making leading to these circumstances. Imagine the beliefs that are guiding those types of choices. Look backward into the past and take responsibility for your choices that have created your present. Recognize that you have full freedom in this moment to begin to make different choices and to create different present moments; ones more to your liking, filled with quality and freedom.

See what choices are available to you right now. Look carefully, because choices, when you are not used to looking for them, can seem to be invisible. They appear not to exist, but in fact they are there. Start with very simple and obvious choices. "What can I choose; what are my options? Could I choose this instead of that? What might happen if I chose that instead of this?" Then take responsibility for both your past and present choices. Visualize the future you desire, imagine the choices necessary to create that future, and take responsibility for beginning that process now. Stop being a victim.

The simple truth is, you were born free; you have free will and choices available to you now. You are responsible for those choices and the circumstances arising from them. *You* choose your life. Look closely into your past, present and future. Examine your beliefs, discover your choices, and create your reality.

Daniel L. DeGoede, Ph.D.

About the Author

Dr. DeGoede is a retired clinical psychologist with over fifty years of providing mental health services to diverse populations with all types of problems. He has devoted his adult life to understanding and communicating the necessary principles of a life of quality.

He is the creator of the therapeutic methodology entitled Belief Therapy® which goes beyond cognitive therapy to examine underlying, unexamined, unconscious core beliefs which are restricting our lives. He believes that "To have freedom, pleasure and quality in our life it is first necessary to explore the inner world of our beliefs."

He is the author of Belief Therapy, A Guide to Enhancing Everyday Life; A Guide to Enhancing Everyday Life, Belief Therapy Volume I Revised; Finding Freedom in Everyday Life, Belief Therapy Volume II; Beliefs for Everyday Life, Words to Live By; Beliefs for Everyday Life, Heartfelt Words.

www.DrDanielDeGoede.com

Belief Therapy
Books by
Dr. Daniel L. DeGoede

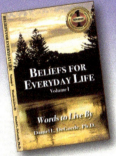 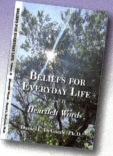

Inspirational Wisdom by Dr. DeGoede

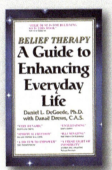 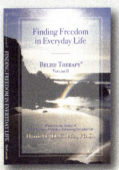 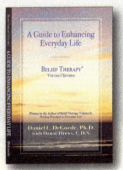

Updated revised versions of Belief Therapy available in print and in ebook.

Buy books online at:
BeliefTherapy.com
DrDanielDeGoede.com

CPSIA information can be obtained
at www.ICGtesting.com
Printed in the USA
BVHW091543030323
659640BV00019B/1218